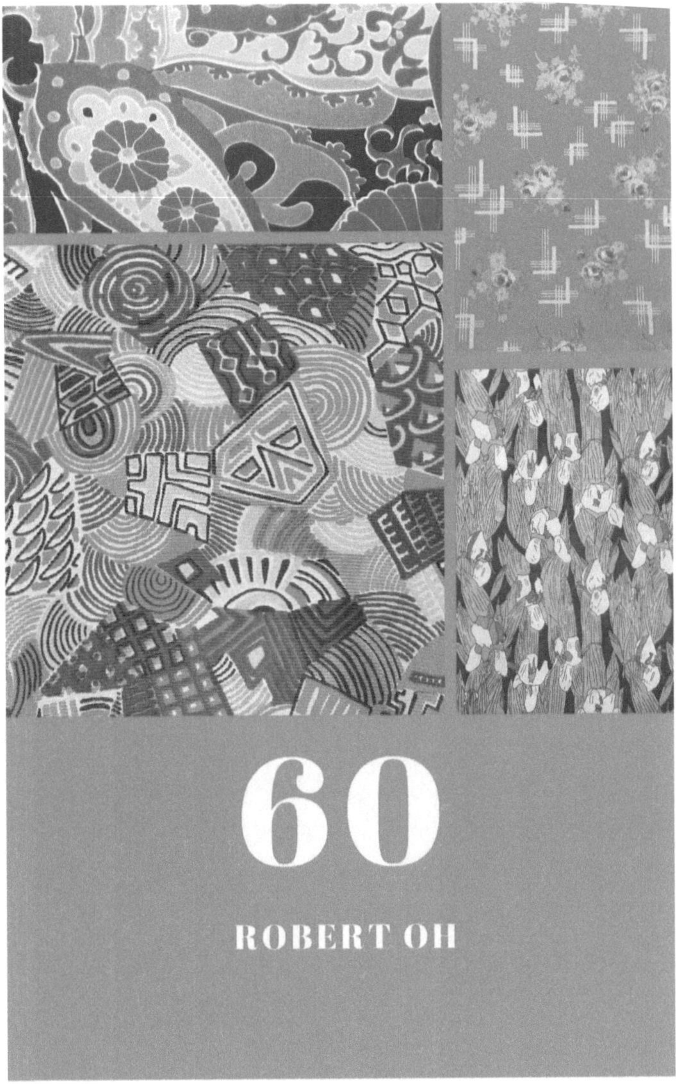

60

ROBERT OH

2

60

Contact Email: oikosbishop@mac.com
Dr. Bob Oh YouTube: https://tinyurl.com/5knavyrw

TABLE OF CONTENTS

BOOK 2 – BEGINNING & THE END   99

INTRODUCTION

"What is a poet? A poet is an unhappy being whose heart is torn by secret sufferings, but whose lips are so strangely formed that when the sighs and the cries escape them, they sound like beautiful music… and men crowd about the poet and say to him: "Sing for us soon again"; that is as much to say: May new sufferings torment your soul." - Søren Kierkegaard

I am celebrating my 61st birthday soon. So before the date - Sep. 24, 2022, I just translate some of my Korean poems into English. Yes – translation of poetry is treason! I published five poetry books in Korean, but none of our children can read Korean. So most likely my grand children and great grand children. I decided to commit the sin of treason and translate some of my published poems into English. It's called, '60,' like Adel's '21.' Enjoy!

BOOK 1 – ON MY WAY TO MOSCOW

BOOK 1 – ON MY WAY TO MOSCOW

In lieu of a Preface:

This year marks the 30th anniversary of immigration to the United States after leaving Korea when I was 12 years old.

Life itself asks questions about our existence.

As an immigrant, I asked endlessly, "Why did God send me to America?" The answer is world mission.

In the mission field I can redeem the suffering I have endured living in a bicultural and a bilingual place. I think our Lord Jesus sent many Koreans to the United States for that purpose.

I had time to organise my life as a father, a pastor, and an individual being on a plane on the way to Moscow, who had lived in the United States for 30 years. It was a time and place where a lot of joy and tears were shed.

I dedicate this collection of poems to members of the Oikos International Mission team.

From Los Angeles
Robert Oh
Spring of 2003

12

THE NIGHT TO MOSCOW

Lord
Are you coming?

This night
is not falling asleep
Moscow must be awake as well.

Tonight
Lord, as you accompany me
I feel secure.

Minus thirty-three degrees
the frozen land,
Let your passion Lord,
The heat of the blood
from the cross
drop
drop
Let them fall.

With you
on our way to Moscow,
this night is beautiful.

My Lord
You too are coming
to Moscow
Aren't you?

A LONG NIGHT

There is...
A night just passes by

I closed my eyes
and saw
a night floating up

Today,
It's bit different
A long night
There's no end
it's hard to see
This Night

There's a white night,
I heard
but it's my first

Just long - too long
Night that feels white
It's a long, long
white night

DREAM

When I dream,
I dream that has no end

Everyone pursue a dream-like life

Endless dreams
I dream of living that kind of life

Break that dream
Before I wake up,
I can't live that dream

If you want to dream,
Have a dream that has an end

What ends in your dream
live it out in real life
Be that kind of life

Delusion - No
Live a real dream

Let's wrap up these endless dreams
Start living that dream that ends

ENDLESS TRIP

I'm heading to Moscow
flight of love

Everyone is sleeping
Coffee keeps me awake
and at work

Moscow
A place with 12 hour difference
To match my body to their time
coffee keeps me up to their day
My nosebleeds proves that it's my night

It's on the other side of the world.

Endless trip
I really can't see the end
But since you're there
I'm flying there with ease

Well done
You will say
To hear your voice
Even on this endless trip
The pinching of joy is what
I have

IF MY LIFE IS A JOKE...

Will it be fun?
If my life is a joke...

Playing all day - every day
fatigue will bring insanity

If only playing is good
God would not have created work

Adam, go out and have fun
        Jumping around like a beast
        Eat all the fruits when you're hungry
        Just pick them at your will
        If you're full and sleepy,
        Under the shade of a tree by the stream,
        Just take a nap

        When you wake up, run around again
        like a beast

Will it be fun?
If my life is a joke?

I think not
Of course not

My life is no joke
Because death ain't funny

PLEASE NOT AT SAUNA ...

At Sauna
Pretend you don't know me

Hey, Pastor - How are you?
Why are you coming to Sauna?

Being shy without any clothes on
I can't pretend that I don't know him
But wearing no glasses
I don't even know who it is

He's not a person with wisdom
to let me pass by
.
"Yes... I just came..."
I stuttered

Why did I come to Sauna?
I'm here to take a bath
not as a pastor
just a dirty guy who needs washing

At sauna
there's no pastor
Just a man
in hot water
a guy full of dirt -
That's all

18

IF YOU...

If you were me,
You
won't respect me

If I were you,
I
won't respect you

Not knowing
That is a good thing

God who knows everything...
Reason for His headache

Even though He knows me,
I has to love me
What pain!

If you were God,
A painkiller as big as Mt. Baekdu
Taken with all the sea water from Namyangman
to deal with all that pain

If you were God,
People like me...
And a guy like you...
You won't be able to forgive

So, God alone...

can carry a cross

20

IF IT IS LOVE...

If you are truly my love,
I should be satisfied,
But why am I so unsatisfied?
Because you are not satisfied!

If it is love,
Please cover it up
Just trust me
Just tell me that I did a good job

Even a grown-up boy
is a child with a runny nose

If it is love,
Just let it pass
I already know before you say it
Before I got the silent treatment
I suffered a great pain

If it is love,
Just love

I want to be with you
Because I am satisfied

with you

HAPPINESS

I'm really happy
I mean it
Lord

Who am I
that you give me such privilege?

Based on what ability
that you gave me this special order?

Who am I
to receive these characteristic

People who live out
how they are formed
are the happiest -
That's what I heard

So
I am really happy

For
as you molded me
I am being used

22

LOVE

Love is not like money
money is spent
to enjoy and to rule

But love is...
like a hot steamed bun
made fresh in the morning

It's delicious when you share it
If you have too much
mold starts to grow

Love is not like money
money makes arrogance
and keeps it grow high

Love
changes a smelly diaper
all night, but with joy
serving a baby

HOWLING...

If howling is a prayer,
did You hear?
Your children's
howling

As the sound of coming waves
waves of tears
angry
sound of howling
prayer

Praying posture of an angel
with hands folded
in perfect serenity
I feel bit annoyed by such image
I must have grown up spiritually

Knowing the depth of life
Can't play around by the shore

Hearing the howling
a prayer like an angel looks foolish
I can not do it

To the sound of the waves,
I pray
No, I pour out my
howling
to You

Did You hear?

IF A WATER BOTTLE COULD SPEAK…

Without saying thank you,
I'm crushing it again
and throw it away

It's just a plastic bottle
but because of it
my thirst was quenched
set free from dehydration
Just a while ago

Looking at the discarded bottle,
I thought it was like me
feeling bit uncomfortable

If God's Words is like living water
surely I
a carrier of these Words
is like that bottle

I put my breath into that crushed water bottle
I decided to carry it around

26

Fight between husband and wife

I was sure of that certainty
of being sure
But I was just checking to be sure

Really, I did nothing wrong
Nothing

Making a resolution
to talk to myself about being sure

Really, what I did was...
Nothing wrong

But why do I feel so yuck
My angle cries
Shooting me with her tear bullets
Ah

Collapsing again
I promised myself
let's make
right right and
wrong wrong
this time

Promising myself
putting two pinkies together

My heart is definitely losing again

I didn't do anything wrong
Other than being a coward who made my wife cry

28

LOVE YOU...

We lived together for a long time
Living with me...
Isn't that love?
I don't ask for more anymore
Thank you
for just living with me

Thank you

Without love,
It wouldn't have been possible

Even if I were her
I don't think I could have done it
If it wasn't for love,

I love my wife
I want to live for the rest of my life

On top of that green grassland
build a picturesque house
Like the lyrics of a song
A silly song
sounds romantic

Probably because
it's just love

Kids these days...

It's was early 70's
I think

Head growing
thinking I'm better than my mom
thinking that I know a lot more things
the year when misunderstood self was born

The 5th grade textbook homework
my mother couldn't solve
surprised by her ignorance

"Kids these days..."
Mom's friends are over
Playing cards
stories are linked together
A remark that comes out time to time
"Kids these days..."

It was last week
December 2002
After 30 years
The youngest one brought her 6th grade textbook
home
Her homework I couldn't solve
surprised daughter teased me
You don't know that?

Just then

My mom spoke through me
"Kids these days..."

A PUPPY BARKS AT NIGHT

It's 2am
A puppy barks at night
A thief is coming
Master, wake up
It's not that kind of barking

Master
I'm hungry
Give me dinner
You forgot
my dinner

Dogs are smart
Watch out for thieves barking
and
Give me food - I'm hungry barking
both sounds 'mung mung' but
different

It's cold, quite annoying hour
to go out to the backyard

I scoop up Puppy Chow and dump
with unkind heart and hands
but he wags his tail and barks
'mung mung'
that means
thank you in puppy language

I had urged to bark
'mung mung' towards the sky

Master, wake up
I'm hungry!

This puppy barked at night

SKIING IN THE MOUNTAINS...

Skiing in the mountains
Surfing in the ocean
Only in Southern California
we can do both

Just thinking about it
can't help but giggle
Put my hands on my mouth
having fun

You could have called me Siberia
You could have called me Cambodia
You could have called me Africa

A city where Korean restaurants are lined up
Offering more delicious Korean food than Seoul.

Skiing in the mountains
I came down to the beach
Surfing
In places like this
God called me as a missionary

Do you favor me?
Thinking about other pastor friends
I can't help but giggle
I can't control myself

Only problem is

I can neither ski nor surf

OUR DAUGHTERS UNDER THE ARMORED CAR...

Is it too much?
Its a mess in Korea,
right now...

Because our daughters
went under the armored car
made in USA

It shouldn't be a mess.

Not just the armored car driver
but the whole country
All the big nosed foreigners
seeking martyrdom
pushing death of all

Eye for an eye
Tooth for tooth
The law of God
they shout

Offer your left cheek
grace of God says

Our daughters
under the armored car
maybe embarrassed
for this riot

Sad and worried

Hating Korea was not motivation
It was just a mistake

* Memo: Korean girls were killed by USA military armored car in Korea.

DREAM VS. REGRET

It's very strange

Dreamers can't achieve their dreams
Only those who live their dreams

Old man who regrets -
just ugly

He says,
was young long ago,
I regret that I did not live boldly

was healthy once,
I regret I did not do my best to serve God

had some money years ago,
I regret not giving away any

It's weird
he who didn't achieve his dream
Hates people who live their dreams

hoping everyone to be
 as ugly as he
regretting their past
living out remaining days
out of jealousy
of those who live their dreams

WHEN YOU MISS AN INNOCENT SMILE

I miss seeing a pollution-free smile
In rural Russia,
I met such a smile.

In a deep Siberian mountains.
Struggling with the cold winter,
Muslim, Orthodox
She fought with Jehovah's witnesses -
One soul. One soul at a time
And taking care of them -
Sister Victoria

Quietly
flows in dark color
A smile around her lips

Like an elementary school girl
Drawing a heart with both hands
kissed me with a blow kiss
a Siberian daughter

I miss that pollution-free smile
I guess that's why I am running to Siberia now

It's probably because of my age

Before I turned 50,
I want to become a grandfather!
I insisted to my eldest daughter
giving healthy pressure

Please don't be an old maid!
One of the hardest parts of the ministry of the second
generation -
Taking care of old maiden
I can't take responsibility because I'm not a Mormon.

Like a joke, demanding grandchildren
to my 18 years old daughter
But in my heart,
it became the truth

It's true
I really miss my grandchildren

You can call me silly
I want to kiss all the kids on the street
I am in trouble

Maybe it's because of my age!

40

WIFE

My wife...
She's really good at praying
When she prays, God...
talks to her

I'm scared
what if He talks about me
I'm in trouble

My wife...
she is so wise
Even though God talked about me
as if nothing
she moves on

I guess she is becoming more like God
He is the one
who lets go and move on

My wife...
she is like God
When I talk to her
I'm scared and nervous...

But she is cute
that is the different
between her and God

Laugh - Ha, Ha

How long has it been?
Laughing foolishly
childishly
For no reason
Laughing - Ha, Ha

Life may have become too serious...

Pastor should
always be so serious?

Ha ha - laugh

It's not so easy

fool

You can't even laugh -
ha ha
How can you share the Good News?

Let's laugh together -
ha ha as we share the Good News!

You aged too quickly,
Pastor!

MISSION TRIP

Why is it so far?

It's not even far away...
13 hours by plane
Someone
took a boat ride for 2 months

Everything he owned
in a box he will be brought back -
coffin
Leaving behind mom, younger sister, and friends...
wailing over his departure

on board a ship
Holding hands with the Lord
Only looking at the Lord
Only loving the Lord
He went a far away place like that

A 13-hour flight -
Why is it so far?

This pastor...
still a long way off

long, long way off

Why is it so far?

Dirty Water is Still Water

Sometimes, I depressed over
my own existence

It's not what it seems

Why does it come short
Why isn't it clean?

Hate - full of it
nervous
 jealous all over

You're the only one who knows

If you pour yourself
Some thirsty pilgrims
will drink

That's the truth

Even if it comes short
Even if it's not clean

Dirty water is still water

44

WHEN THE FISH TASTES GOOD

Seeing that the fish is delicious
I guess my life is delicious as well

one of my father's cousin's cousin
had fish bone stuck in his throat and died
on account of his death
I could only eat canned mackerel...
grew up without knowing the taste of fish

inadvertently placed in my mouth
a piece of fish
started to melt
sweet-tasting

Look at this
One who wouldn't let me eat fish
My dad is gone
And now I am of his age
myself - as that old man's
first encounter with real fish

Children!
Eat the fish
It's so delicious

Seeing that the fish is tasty
I guess life is delicious now

But I Pray fervently

that bones won't get stuck in their throat

46

IS IT TRUE?

What is true?
Is there really a fake?
If there's a fake,
Is that a real fake?

The word 'real' itself
Is it real?

What is real, really?

If there's really no real,
What is true?

I really have no idea

True!

what is real?
I need someone to tell me this, really
it is necessary

True!

I am not joking!

Don't laugh!

THE DAY I CAUGHT HIM

Make sure to hide
I can see your hair
He was playing hide and seek

He hid so well
That guy...
I couldn't see his face

Although it was hide-and-seek
The situation was always
a 100-meter dash

impossible to spare
wild run -
It was the same game

Make sure to hide well
I can see your hair
said the voice of a child
But a middle-aged man -
That's what he looked like

When his heart was having
what we call 'Attack'

I got him

And he caught me

AT THE END OF MY 40 YEARS

Expensive hotel room
With Priceline.Com
at a very low price for a day

in a place like this
I can have a day retreat
proud of myself

Expensive life
did I sell it at very low price?
I don't know if I lived
my 40 years of life
selling as a bargain

The finishing 40 years
is the beginning of another 40 years
but creaking sound of
past 40 years
I'm more concerned

Lord!
After the next 40 years
would I use
Heaven.Com
to find a room?

But God...

But God
The difference between embarrassment and absurdity
You know that, right?

When a dog bites a person,
one gets flustered

When a person bites a dog,
We say it's absurd

People eat dogs
Eating dog soup

But God,
You're the one who gave us
all animal as food so we can
Eat them

eating the food You gave them
Why some big noses folks get
frustrated?

God
I'm really flustered

You know the difference between
frustration and absurdity,

RIGHT?

Why pastor?

Lord,
I really don't know

As a pastor
for studying the Bible
gets salary
so how's that hard life
I really don't understand

for praying
for proclaiming the Word
for loving our neighbours
You guaranteed our livelihood

for working hard
people invite you to their house
feeding delicious food
blessings from the Lord
I got'em for free
so I give as much as I want

when we say good bye
people give a white envelop
filled with cash
to Thank You for all I do
& That's what I do.

Why, pastors -
do you say it's a difficult job?

Maybe when the truth is revealed
you are afraid that
too many
will become our competitors

I am not sure
but maybe that's what it is

THERE THERE

Someone said to me,
Go there
So I did

place like this
is really the best place!

If it's the best place
I should go
and experience
unwilling to lose to lose to others
I to to
places like that
always dragged around

And to someone else...
I repeat the same talk
place like that
is really the best place!

Really there was a place like that,
they say and they run in line
to go there

All are like acorns!

I'll go there too
Because I have to measure my height
against the other guy

Acorns
love to measure their
height
with one another

THERE IS NO REASON FOR SORROW

It's just sadness
no need a reason

I just wanted to cry
I'm crying

If you cry
you feel refreshed
I heard that inside person gets healthier

It's just sadness
for no reason

Being sad without reason
There's no reason to be sad

today
I'm just going to cry my eyes out
Sadness has no reason
Tears...
one by one
with each its own stories
hits the pavement

Hey,
Let's cry our hearts content

There is no reason for sorrow

BEGINNING OF THE DAY

My hands are shaking
All night long
I wrote a poem
One, two, three...
38!

today
day at Moscow begins
a long night
and a morning that follows...
Refreshing

Like a soldier in a war
After shooting all night
hands tingling
Like that soldier
today
this day is

STARTING

WHEN LIFE IS SAD

My mom said,
Sometimes life is sad...

To be honest, when I heard that
I laughed at her

It's so nice
It's so exciting
We're young and all the days are fresh

So what's so...
sad?

The day that all of them left me -
wife and the first and the second,
on a short mission trip
Third, to a ski trip...
The comrade who ran with me for 12 years...
to his own pasture...
disciples I raised to better teachers
few of the sheep who said loved me
took off the skin and left the flock
as pack of wolves

A day when life felt filthy and sad

I
like my mother
who said sometimes life is sad

shed her tears
sitting alone in a hotel room
with a loud voice
I cried

THE PRAISE I GAVE YOU THAT NIGHT

Late at night
I was still able to play guitar

No more finger pointing
No one to point to

Reaching the point of embarrassment
how much complaining can one do?

At that moment...
Prayer that does not requests

The prayer with one tune...
shriek
crawling
like web
sigh
on the way out

praising you with
most beautiful
new song
a fragrant memorial offering
night of the fire.

transcendent
peace and joy
embraced me that night

That night
triumphant through praise

in a prison-like hotel room
listening to the praises of Paul and Silas

PAIN OF JOY

I was completely fooled
There was no joy of pain
Even though there's a pain of joy,

Because the pain itself
extinguish the joy
There is no joy of pain

Joy is
to forget pain
like a medicine root

The pain makes suffering
flavoured like seasoning

from now on
I won't fall for it

Rather than the joy of suffering,
all for the pain of joy

I'll bet on that
everything
I own

IT'S JUST SHARING

It's nothing
I'm just giving it all out

Master
left it up to me
to share it with so and so
So I'm just giving it all out

Love?
No
I'm just giving it all out

Joy?
No
I'm just giving it all out

Dedication?
No
Master who gave it to me told me to give it all out
So I'm just giving it all away

It's nothing
I'm just giving all of it

What belonged to Master
For Him
by His ability

distributing it all away

62

that's all

BIRDS...

Even with just two notes, the birds
are very good at singing

Even without the lyrics
they sing praise songs

all the birds
spray the poo all over
as they fly around

Birds fall only with God's permission
experience the benefit of
falling to the ground

Birds are really
loved by
God

maybe because they are
flying in the air
closer to Him

APPLE

Reverend.. Moksanim!
a Russian woman following me
calling me in Korean

She offers me an apple
to me who looks like a snowman
all covered up
walking in snow

the snow-white hands says
heart warming
"Thank you"

Winter in Siberia is severe
there's nothing to eat
a new student receives one fruit each day
like vitamins
And she is giving that to me

She said she was grateful
to receive my teaching
and gave up her vitamin

I put it on the desk
This apple that I can't eat
grateful deeply from my heart

I have many people who want to
give this apple to

When I go back to America
I should send each of them
a box of apples

Minus Thirty-Three Degrees

It was really cold

the first day of a Moscow seminary lecture
on the way to the early morning prayer
I met Mr. minus 33 degrees

It started to all freeze
warm breath
The runny nose
Even the tears in my eyes
The warmth of your body and
The confidence that I felt as well

Mr. -33 Degrees
stole everything

Put my hands, feet, and hair
crumpled
waddling
started walking
like a turtle

I met him at dawn
Mr. - 33 degrees
he was no joke

Birch Tree

Tall birch tree
are like a Russian woman

at a slender height
curved hair

like many Russian women
walking on snow

When spring comes
The naughty boys
with a knife
cuts into them
for them to spill the water of life

collected
in the bottle
feminine moist -
water of life

A sweet tasting water
I've tried it
last spring

Was it like a forbidden kiss
with a Russian woman?

Waiting for spring
as snow continues to fall

on a Russian woman tree

Dogs' Dialect

Korean dogs bark - Mung Mung
American dogs bark - Ruf Ruf
Russian dogs bark - Gaf Gaf

Do dogs have a native language?

When a cat barks,
Is it a bilingual cat?

In a place where many ethnic groups gathered
I told them
Let us bark in our dog's dialect

Mung Mung, Ruf Ruf, Gaf Gaf...
Really
it was a mess

Even so
for a while
in one's own dog's dialect
we were happy

I came to USA when I was 12
I've lived for 30 years

My dog
oddly enough
barked
Mung Mung

ONE, TWO, THREE...

One, two, three...

The water in the bathhouse smells good

When I was 12 years old
I left Korea
But that old man is here again

One, two, three...
counting in a sad tone

My chubby son jumps into the hot water

Dad, why are you counting one, two, three...
in such a funny tone

Well, the bathhouse really needs a grandfather who counts
the 'han' of Korea
in a hot bath
as anger boils within

The heat of sauna
cools down with a waterfall shower
as a new young grandfather
leaves the bathhouse

FRAGMENTS OF THOUGHTS

They talk of love
Hands of God
The way of Love
Can NOT be contained

Lord, my path of life
One road I want to race
There is mother waiting in love
One foot lifted, facing the
World on her back

Like a crow crying on top of an evergreen
Crying without tears in time

There is no black rainbow they say
But home without love hangs on the sky

Tomorrow comes as it drags its
Feet on the ground

* 5th Epipodo Literature Poetry Publication Dr Jonah
Back Pg 79

EARLY MORNING

I look at the Lord
in the early morning

Appreciation, praise, joy

darkening are
painful relationships
distorted relationships
passing in front of me
like a phantom vision

pray that I won't be attached to the
luggage I have to leave behind

I won't bet my life on these
dead &
dry
memories of the past
which chose to die

Lord,
Please revive it new

Everything goes into the darkness
as I to start run again...

Please revive it new

Early in this morning

AIRPLANE

Apples are delicious
delicious is banana
Bananas are long
long is a train
train is fast
fast is an airplane
Airplanes are high
high is Mt. Baekdusan!

With my childhood friends
We had a silly imagination
About high and fast airplane

Now
Sitting on the airplane that I imagined as a child
high up in the sky
remembering our childhood

Delicious apples
became an airplane
carrying me over Mt. Baekdusan
My life will undergo
many changes

Toward the top of Mt. Baekduan
its soaring

Lord,
Give me the wings of an eagle

So that we can fly together...

PRACTICE

My youngest' butt
cute
touch and kiss
the first one says its gross

When child thinks dad's touch are gross
are you old enough to know about life?

endless practice continues in life
don't judge success while practicing

a bird flying in the air is also practicing
even a toddler walking
Mom who gave birth is also practicing raising a child
When will I know when to stop kissing my child's butt?

Everything is just practice...

My life...
approaches me day by day
they are precious as my youngest' butt

AUGUST 10, 1999

Han Areum

Under the scorching sun of Almaty, Kazakstan,
a Korean daughter

Her name was Han Areum

"I'm Korea" And spoke Russian
"I'm Han Areum" And spoke Russian
She showed her four fingers
and said he was four years old

Why does a little girl I've never seen
reaches my heart so deeply?

here in this poor country
in a foreign land -
great suffering is expected
this beautiful Korean daughter
will live - here

May you live with the blessings of the Lord always
Every day, every day, the love of the Lord be Han
Areum

leave the spirit of Korea Han Areum
on this Kazakstan land

My dear future daughter

August 12, 1999

Pessimism & Hope

South Korea
shifting back and forth
it is lost
and at a loss for words

taxi is racing mad
as it's running to death
At Dongdaemun & Namdaemun
an enthusiastic crazy making
is taking place now

Itaewon is reeling from alcohol
an old man picking cigarette butts
staggered by IMF

When will Korea comeback?
When will you comeback?

Lord,
Please let your Korea
comeback

August 20, 1999

SOLITUDE

You should not feel lonely if you have God
So I preached
This winter, when my whole family left
I feel lonely next to God

The Emptiness in
Adam's Chest
Sadness in
God's heart

Because of loneliness,
Eve was made
now that she is gone
he becomes lonely

as long as God is around
there should be no pain
impossible
So I preached
this impossible was made possible
the emptiness
today
when Eve left

God, I am sorry
but
I miss my wife!

I know you are with me...
Even though I knew that Lord you are with me,
But I still miss
I can't help but miss my wife

December 3, 2002

6.25

the bitterness of war
tears scattered in the War Museum
the eyes of children who first saw 6.25

My wife cried
I cried, too

the pain of war -
neither poverty nor death
but pain of hatred

It's 6.25

It's flesh

under the guise of a human being
like an animal
it was their yuk?

And also my flesh

the enemy of flesh and blood
It's 6.25

not wishing for
days without war
for our children,
but victory over flesh

ugly and evil
of flesh
to be victorious over
I pray

8/24/99

LOVE

I saw love

unwritten
unspeakable

running through the streets of Seoul
crossing Namdaemun Market
climbing the Namsan Tower,
strolling through the folk village
riding on the north-south highway...
I saw that love

to remind you of love
to erase the debt of love
the Apostle of Love's love
poured it from the bottom of his heart

Love without boundaries...

I felt that love

8/25/99

ANSWER!

What's this?
Patty asks

Everything she sees
What is it?
She asks

The subway that's running away like it's being chased,
And people bumping into you don't say sorry
On a two lanes road
three cars are tangled in Seoul
the bulgogi burger she had at the Highway terminal
snack bar
freshly baked walnut cake
Ulleungdo squid - grilled with peanut butter,
sticky Korean affection
All of them . . .

What's this?

The answer to that question I pray is
Love

I hope...

8/26/99

AT THE ORCHARD

A 5,000 won for one pear
opens like the sea

If you touch,
it drops

each child took one
we got 20,000 won worth of pear

popping
in the mouth
a wave of sugar water

after a year's hard work
it's the sweat of grandfather

salty sweat
tastes like sweet candy

it's worth 5 million won each
stomach full of lessons in one pear

8/27/99

ON MY WAY HOME

joy of giving birth
after 12 hours of pain,
the joy of liberation - freedom

kids are bored
twisting them in pain of boredom
Even the flickering movies in front of them
can not entertain them

from exhaustion
my love
leaned over and use my shoulder as her pillow
dreaming smog of LA

once again, going through the pain of birth
together

on the plane to LA
Why is it going so slow?

8/29/99

86

A JOURNEY TO ETERNITY

Starting at Miami
going to Orlando
on a long-train ride
long time going

abandoned on the dining-room floor
are our useless pride

masks that come off one by one
humility of contradiction vanishing
burst of laughter
not even trying

the summer rain in Orlando
falls like the laughter,
with the excitement of autumn
Harvest

on a long train
connected to a long long time

my dear eternal comrades...

10/3/ 99

Laying of hands

What are you going to become when you grow up, kid?

child's knee
sobbing with tears

the crossing point of
fear of the future and
conviction of faith
marked by her tears

dream of her future
passing like a cloud above her

the storm of chaos today
shakes the past and the future

but time such as this
in prayer and by prayer
it's taking roots

like a tree transplanted by the stream
pray that fruits will be harvested on that tree

enduring breaking pain against the ground,
from the loneliness of being alone...

What are you going to become when you grow up, kid?

seeds of the tears that you are sowing now

88

will become a harvest in the future

you live out your dream like a cloud in reality
calmness of the wind will shake you

on the back of my hand
tears of desperation
are sobbing

10/7/99

Grandpa Samson

Two eyes that Samson lost
because he lost the vision from God
I shouted

this generation that God wants to use
cool looking like Samson's long hair
even if Samson-like power is lacking
do not lose the vision from God

my desperate cry from the pulpit
it rings as a prayer in the wilderness

not as the tragic hero
nor a tragic generation
only fear God
serve only God
give glory back to God
my sons and daughters

insulting Grandpa Samson
I challenge you

trying not to lose my own eyes
shouting with my eyes wide open

10/9/99

OLD PEOPLE

They'll never be like that
I thought
But they've become old people

endless love
giving absolute love
they gave us

drive carefully
take care of your health
endless chattering
talk and talk
look like and sound like
old people

When did they become like that?
Their past looks wonderful rather than the future
sudden realisation

happy to see my baby becoming a teenager now
even this father
became old

drive carefully
take care of your health
endless chattering
talk and talk
look like and sound like
old man

Elisa will say, "Come on, old man!"
and will wipe off her tears

They'll never be like that
I thought
But they've become old people
like an old man of my future

11/28/00 @ Sacramento

FAITH

knowing ...
we won't walk on that path again

It was as transparent as a marble
certainty of the future
but it wasn't clear
and we won't go back that path again

we decided
not knowing
but walking only on that path
relying on Him

knowing ...
on that path
we won't walk on that path again

6/1/00 @ Korea written with Jenny

STONE

sitting

sitting because it can't stand up

But
He who sits to rest,
to rest to stand is at peace

There is a stone sitting outside the door
in order to shout and stand
when the horn of heaven rings

rest, rest
be at peace

* Epippodo Poetry Society Publication 1999.

94

WIND AND THE WISH

Run with the wind
Go after the time like flesh and blood
Your ideal that goes up to the sky
dream them up like millions of balloons
sending all your dreams upwards

wind is blowing

free
like a blowing wind
this world is vast
run as fast as you can
following His hand
like a tree transplanted at His stream

walk all over the world
but stay there
in His hands

place where the Holy Spirit blows

place where wind and the wish meet

1/13/01

MOUNTAIN

climbed a mountain
taking forever
but it is so small

now coming down

next day, it looks impossible to climb
It's a long way up
but climbed it again today
taking forever
but it is so small
coming down again

time goes by
climbing up and down...

The joy of climbing
The joy of coming down
started to match

deep in my heart
under a cliff
I found such mountain

* During Fasting 40 days in 1999

To Exist

Flying over Canada
I feel lonely all of a sudden

It's really just me

When the word "alone" is comfortable,
I become really lonely

There are no clouds today
There are no birds
Where am I flying alone?

at a faster pace than the wind blows
with a loud noise in one's head
Am I even going somewhere?

Losing all 5 Senses
floating in the air
like the philosophy's guinea pig,
do I exist?

The feeling of being lonely is not in a non-existing state,
since I feel it
Loneliness proves that I exist
Isn't it the real beginning?

Adam was lonely so Grandma Eve was made
Loneliness produced another existence

at this lonely moment
I meet myself

as I fly over Canada

February 11, 2002:
Going to a revival meeing in Gwanglim Church of
Canada

SHEEP

Live like a sheep
wind blowing onto your soul
The world full of our Lord

naked we come
and naked we will go back

Stay alone, but be together

Remembering the past
yearning for the future
and stay true to the present

Always remain in the Lord's heart

Sorrow will come as sorrow
Joy will go as joy

be still in the Lord
in a silent praise,
Sing a song to Him

like a sheep
always remain the soul in His arms

* Rewriting Ryu Si-hwa's 'Wild Grass' from my perspective.

BOOK 2 – BEGINNING & THE END

In lieu of a Preface:

Only one life
T'will soon be past
Only what's done for Christ will last
To me to live is Christ
To die is gain.

Our lives begin and end. Just as our God himself said that He is alpha and omega, our lives have a beginning and an end. I pray that the moments between the beginning and the end can be devoted to our Lord Jesus and we live only for Him.

I would like to express my warm thanks to Choi Yoonjung for helping me publish this book and my sister Oh Somi for correcting all the poems and always supporting me as a poet. Sincere thanks for 'Faith and Gisung Publishing House' for publishing this book for Cambodia and Siberia mission work without fee.

This little collection of poetry book is dedicated to my wife, Jenny, who has been with me for 20 years. Pray that the companionship of love that began with her will last till the day we meet our Lord Jesus.

Robert Oh
In the spring of 2004 at Los Angeles

THE END OF THE UNIVERSE

going to sleep
to travel to the end of the universe

children I loved
teachers I admired

on a coal furnace
sticky smell
piling up on top
coming out of lunch boxes

It was warm
furnace and memories

my first love at
third grade
elementary school
Lee Soonja

Things like that are trifle
you say

but
i have to travel to the end of the universe
to be there again

It was the beginning of
innocence

and also the end of
innocence

No
end of that universe

Name in Three Alphabet

father's name in three alphabet
at his cemetery lot
dizzy with dust and weeds
wiped it with my hands
I don't have any paper

father's name in three alphabet
crouched down next to him
I watch countless cars
briskly passing by
on 605 Freeway

Where are they all heading
speeding mad?

going such a hurry
when it's over
all
will
end up
here
as
a name in three alphabet

father's name in three alphabet
my name in three alphabet
children's name in three alphabet
list them up in order
in rows

And then try to
wipe them with my hands

names written in air
they don't erase easily

Lord's Day, 1

high sky
as birds chirp

happy hearts
sad hearts
coming together

to the house of God
returning
a large flock of sheep

a white sheep
a black sheep
a crippled sheep

from a distance
looks wonderful
and beautiful

but near them
The smell of sheep is real

yet better than wonderful sight afar
smelly sheep
became lovelier

shepherds
and flock of sheep needs to be together

106

under the high sky
underneath the flying birds
Some may
say, "it's beautiful!"

this morning
on this Lord's day

SEASON

autumn without leaves
thirty times
autumn in Southern California
coming slower because of Palm trees?

snow-free winter
thirty times
winter in Southern California
coming slower because of Palm trees?

365 times thirty times
the season that only comes only by numbers
spring, summer, autumn, and winter
passing only as number

today,
the number on my calendar
red has merged
color of autumn leaves

Bloody Tears

Forgiveness saves me
Unforgiveness nailed everyone

the Lord of the Cross
begs to
forgive

a cross
only as an accessory

till the end
we can not forgive
we can not love

can not love
because can not forgive

Is it a prayer or a curse?
prayer
without forgiveness
is all in vain

the cross
dripping blood

AS TEARS

The End of Everything

The end of everything
So beautiful

Creation:
the sun crossing the horizon
So beautiful

Creator:
"It is finished!"
That last breath
given to sinners
beautiful as well

Creature:
Adam's last day
The day he was embraced by the new Garden of Eden
it was also a beautiful day

The end of everything
are all beautiful

Daisy

my favorite flower
Daisy

First, Daisy is a flower

Second, Daisy is cheap

Third, one Daisy alone
is not beautiful

many love
rose
as it is beautiful alone
but
such ignorance of beauty
cause such misunderstanding
of what beauty really is

one Daisy alone
is not beautiful
but just lonely

Daisy only among many daisy
starts to shine

I like Daisy

PRAYER

Dear Lord,
may pure heart and softness
become one
like now

seeing the lightening
as your fire stick
cloud
as your breath
not as electricity
not as vaporise steam
consider all of it as
yours

may such heart come back to me

just once
even for a moment

let
my heart
and I
become one...

Dear Lord,
I pray that to you

112

GRACE

rain, wet me

although a light
gotten too used to the darkness

neat and tidy
outer shell
please wash it

wet me with rain

it is light in fact
but indistinguishable from darkness

this ugly outer shell
wash it clean please

rain, wet us all

sweet rain of grace

AT STARBUCKS

the dusk
had come before I knew it

even before the warmth
of my latte leave

Espresso is too strong
Cappuccino is served too little
if it is the same price
Latte is
full of healthy milk
It was my choice drink

It's time to get up
It's time
yet I can't leave this place
What's going on?

Until the latte is finished?
price paid for a seat not complete?

until the dusk of the evening comes
until it's darkness without regrets
come I shall hold on

Oh, my
without being greedy
I should get up now

114

LORD'S DAY, 2

there is a station called
Sunday

We are travellers
on the same path
gather to this station

each one
getting on a train of their own destiny
going everywhere

Of course, there's no fare
a ticket called faith
you must show

If you go in
to a train better than Saemaeul train
full of
fluffy chair

If you go to the station called Sunday,
take the best looking train
going furthest
the most expensive-looking one
the kind of train
that you ride with faith

don't worry about the fare
ride with faith

faith is enough

Memory

Don't you remember
A day in September?

one day in autumn
on that day
a day that became beautiful
after time has passed

The time passed - now and then
made it beautiful -
that person
and there

That's weird
They're both H_2O
but
time past builds up like snow
time now flows like a water

Don't you remember
A day in September?
May your day in September
Be your day today

Keep this in mind
in the past September
that one day...

on that day

that day
may it be today....

118

PRAYER

Until we compared
we were happy

Lord,
return my heart that did not compare
let me live in happiness in life before comparing

Lord,
Eve compared with You
she sowed seeds of sin in the Garden of Eden

Cain compared with Abel
picked up a rock
covering with the blood of the curse
once the land of blessing

Saul compares with David
became miserable
Even though he was a king,
tricked by the snake that stole Eve's heart

That snake never stops whispering
to me as well

Whispering
Compare...

Lord,
I pray

that we won't compare

With this right now, with this time, with this itself,
that I will be satisfied

Lord,
Until we compared
we were happy

THE WIND

wind is a black cloud's
flirtatious person

When wind passes by
dark clouds arrive

clouds pass by
pouring the rain

rain penetrates deep into the ground

warmth of the sun
make green shoots
pout

Spring has come before I knew it

wind brings spring
like a flirtatious person

CHANGE

day by day
days connect as everyday

every moment
connect
by hour by hour

in this breathtaking life
in this present continuity
I am
connected with every day and
every moment
without any defence

my today changes
as today becomes tomorrow's yesterday
tomorrow connects me to the future
I am
changing
as a result

from day to day
everyday after everyday.

Every moment
by the hour
I have been connected

a key to change is
me

A MOTIVE FOR WRITING POETRY

If there is an end, I will not write poetry
It's majestic to have an end

a poem written knowing the end
a poem written at the end
a poem written with a feeling of the end
poems written at the end are all different
but
It all ends

poems that acknowledge the end
and poems that interprets in vain are different

admission is noble but
emptiness is sadness
for I feel lonely

there's an end
so I write a poem again today

THE BEGINNING AND THE END

without beginning or end
life that's being regenerated
as a cow and a horse
is like a fog

At a close distance
and far away
without knowing who it is
without knowing where it is
being bottled in a fog

life is not like that

Alpha and Omega

Like Alpha our lives begin
Like an omega our lives end

When there's nothing more to be desired on this earth
anymore
And when it is decided
fog clears
so I walk alone on a trail

And being alone
I'm not
finally
not lonely

HIDE AND SEEK

It wasn't two, it was three
Me, Myself & I

To become one
The hide-and-seek continued...

Secret dreams
In a reality where you hide yourself,
sky and
Water
Love and
stars
All of them
to a place that all flows into one

there
two become one
Three of us became one

The game of hide and seek
is finally over

126

WHAT'S LEFT?

at the University of San Diego
the eldest daughter in school
Put her in the dorm

The day after I came back,
"How are you?" I called her
My daughter said,
'Everything is FINE!'

'Everything is FINE?'

How can everything be FINE?
you should miss my mom and dad
You should have to said, "I feel like dying!"
That's right
How can Everything is FINE?
My oldest daughter, Elisa, made us feel sad

raising daughters are wasting of time
someone tries to comfort me
I said YES
in response

then a thought came
very long time ago,
one day in September
I remembered the conversation I had with my mother
at the Berkeley dorm
'I am FINE, Mom… Everything is FINE!'

Your mother must have been very sad

I made up my mind that day
Be nicer to my wife...

What's left is
are not sons and daughters

Who, Who?

Who are you…
Who, Who
Who, Who?

The song I used to sing when I was young
was a huge hit

these days
I think deeply about
their prophetic lyrics

Really
Who am I?
Who, Who
Who, Who?

becoming more desperate
for an answer

I must be
little bit more
mature
now

COMPANION

we are traveling

maybe she's snoring because she's tired
my wife
opening my eyes,
worrying

at the Waikiki hotel room,
I'm spending the night with pastor friend

Rather than sleeplessness,
I miss my wife even more

without knowing the time difference
I got a call at 6 a.m
another friend New York

recognising that voice,
I was happy to talk to him

Whispering, holding hands over the phone on bed
I miss voice of my wife even more

a companion in life journey

As a punishment for coming to Waikiki alone
God makes me more
lonely

130

As expected, solo trips are the best in life
No

I have to do it with her

In the sound of my friend's snoring,
I miss my wife

GOLF

All the pastors
I've met
successful
excellent ones
play golf

I haven't met him yet
a successful
pastor -
Reverend Billy Graham, too
I heard plays golf
especially with the Presidents

Hum,
because I do not play golf
I haven't succeed yet?

Success
Is it 'Holy Ball?'

A pastor I met in Hawaii
I said I played 77
I asked what does that mean?
He said you're so '7 7' clumpsy.
How can you not know even that much?

To be a good pastor
May be I should play golf?

Maybe I will be 'Holy Ball'

CRAB DEATH

flesh light in front
we ran barefoot

screaming
at midnight
a hunt for crabs on the beach in Hawaii
began

seeing light,
mom crab is running
dad crab
and baby crabs

in the clutches of the running youths
caught in a blue plastic barrel
taken prisoner

hey, let's do some exercise under the moon light
such an innocent game we played
but several crabs died

grilled over an open fire
mouth watered for
hunters

literally they
experienced crab death

AT THE WAIKIKI BEACH

tens of millions of tourists
passed through
Waikiki Beach

tens of millions times
the waves
rushed in

countless times
the wind and the revolution of the whole earth
brings
waves waves waves

waves like these
we have in California, too
an ignorant tourist said

did they hear him?
I thought they would get mad if they heard him
I talked even louder

these Waikiki Beach's waves
they are so beautiful
they are so very unique

Even after rushed in tens of millions of times,
once again, a wave
waved 'Aloha'

and pushed out

PRAYER OF BECOMING

We pray because we need
We cry because we hurt
We are what we pray

Each prayer becomes me

Let me pray myself to a
Being, making and molding
Each character
Fashioning them into a
Being

Prayer of becoming...
Lord, that's what I want.

Lord,
I hope my life will be shaped by prayer
let it not be - 'oh give it to me'
but 'oh, let it become'

being completed little by little
through prayer

desperate
to become a butterfly
struggling to become
a butterfly

a prayer that's making

of becoming

THE HORIZON

not far away
but near by
there is this horizon
for me

just to look at
such a horizon
is there to just look at

this horizon is most beautiful,
when the sun makes a mad dash
and sink
shouting
red and yellow
as it sinks

such a
horizon
day after day every
day
dances
in my pocket

PROMISE

A promise made with pinkies
It's too weak
It's so childish
promises are not made with your fingers

A promise made with heart
always lies
It's so fake
promises are not made by heart

A promise made with my lips
It's always light
talking is cheap
promises are not made with lips

A promise made with prayer
It's always honest
Promises are made only by prayer

These promised are made
to God in fear
whom should be feared

* In memory of Mrs. Esther Ahn who guided me to this
truth

DIRECTOR

Lord
Look at the Southern California

This place became so famous without you
tens of thousands
Come to see Hollywood
Come to Disneyland

In search of dreams
come to find love
and You're so obscure here

like an extra
in a movie
your name
appears among so many

Lord
please
become the director

Please write a script
as you wish
and direct
as you will

And Lord

use me
as your
eternal extra

142

PRAISE

praise you
I praise you
with all of my heart
with all of my body
in one voice
I praise you

Praise of the Mute
in their own voice
resonates from the bottom of their heart

no eyes
no hands and feet
The praise of body-less self

You're the only one who sees
you know
you feel

to those who does not praise
all are ungrateful
for those who praise
all are praise itself

I praise you
Lord
Just you
I sincerely
praise you

A DAY THAT THE CORE FALLS APART

time and time again
There's a day when the core collapses

Why is that?

If you say that there is no reason,
It would be a lie

probably someone
some incident
some situation
mocked me
and ridiculed me

although it is not that difficult

life -
color of it
thought of it
and
even breathing seems difficult
on that day the core collapses

I'm glad I wasn't there
at the center of the core

144

Yosemite Grizzly Giant

One scholar said its 3000 years old
Another scholar claimed 2000
Hello Grizzly
Hello Grizzly
The day Jesus was born
What did you dream about?

To see Jesus in Maria's arms
Did you grow tall?

Yosemite
in the forest of Mariposa
Goliath size
Giant Trees

hearing the shout of
Sequoia trees
lying dead
here and there

Four million people are coming
per year
stepping on your roots
make you fall

Hello Grizzly
Hello Grizzly

Live a long life
and welcome
our Lord's return

A NIGHT BREEZE

dark night
opens its window
in secret

drinking the rushing night breeze

My heart
is with the wind
of the spring

This body has
nowhere to go
so it stands alone
at this night

A WOODEN DOLL

It doesn't move,
but it isn't dead

It doesn't speak
but it isn't a mute

like death
like a mute
It just stays quiet

Like a wooden doll

In the Woods

Not a moment of
hope and despair
in such a state of pause

not a moment of joy for sure
meet a woman
who appears in the woods

one who swallows your dreams
a woman of scattered hair

in the woods
days
are thicker and longer
than in the city

The sunlight
The smell
even the thought

my meeting continues
with that woman
in the woods

How life lives

We eat death to live
Cooking starts with killing
If there's no death, life is dead
Death saves our lives

To live and die is the same thing
Life feeds on death

SUMMER AT TRENG VILLAGE

It's hot
boiling
and annoying summer in Cambodia

In this hot and boiling place,
what does people with leprosy
do?

grandfather digging the ground
with hands without fingers
Did they used their fingers as fertiliser?
or used them as seeds?

If you plant your fingers,
What will grow?

looking back on the
hungry past
here at hot and boiling place
future is being planted

Night

by the window
seeped in
a dark night

quietly
softly
surrounding me

from the tip of my head
to the bottom of my feet
erasing
everything

like a pencil eraser
night
erases

my shining eyes
have flown away

I can see the dark
darkness itself

the madness night
begins

I
quietly
erase my ears

erasing even
the night

DEATH AND LIFE

by death
life dazzles -
transformation

to die is gain
someone said

emancipation
from painful
breathless days
belongs to death itself.

Rather than living with anxiety,
in between life and death
by dying
I chose a deeper life

In Seo Jung Joo's poem, 'Green Day' -
The green leaves gets tired and turns to the autumn red

Did it die from the exhaustion of life?

do we say them to be beautiful
death of green leaves

by death
life dazzles

Jump!

*Pearling Kierkegaard's words

Who is a poet?
He is an unhappy man who conceals
profound anguish in his heart.
Yet whose lips are so formed that
as sighs and cries pass over them…
they sound like beautiful music.

"Love does not alter the beloved",
he says,
"it alters you."
Love is all, it gives all, and it takes all.
So, don't forget to love yourself.
Don't become indifferent.
Don't become a stranger…
At the bottom of enmity between strangers
lies indifference.

Be free!
Be that self which one truly is.
You will lose control, do not fear anxiety…
Anxiety is the dizziness of freedom.

During the first period of a man's life,
the greatest danger is not to take the risk.
Not to be anxious…
Not to be free…

You are free, indeed. Yet...
How absurd you are!
You never use the liberties you have, and...
You demand those you do not have.
You have freedom of thought, but...
You demand freedom of speech,
freedom from finance,
freedom from social injustice.

Ah, because you who as a physical being always
turned toward the outside,
thinking that your happiness lies outside,
you finally turn inward and discover that
the source is within you.
Face the facts of being who you are inside...
for that is what will change who you are outside.

Jump! Have faith in God...
If I am capable of grasping God objectively,
I do not believe,
but precisely...
because I cannot do this...
I must believe.
I must jump!

The paradox is really the pathos of intellectual life
and just as only great souls are exposed to passions...
it is only the great thinker who is exposed to what I call
paradoxes,
which are nothing else than grandiose

thoughts in embryo.
It is in this imperfection of everything
You can attain your desire -
by passing through the opposites.

Take away paradox from the thinker...
and you have a professor.

So, Jump! Have faith in yourself...
Become that self which one truly is.
It is so hard to believe because
it is so hard to... obey.
Faith is the highest passion you will ever experience.

Faith is a snare,
you cannot have it, without being caught.
You cannot have faith in such a way that
you catch it,
but only in such a way that it catches you.

So, Jump! And live your life to the fullest...
Life can only be understood backwards;
but it must be lived forwards.
Life's hidden forces can only be
discovered by living.

The highest and most beautiful things in life...
are not to be heard about,
nor read about,
nor seen,
but to be lived.

Purity of heart is to will one thing...
To be that Individual..
Desire it. Think it. Meditate it...
Our life always expresses the result of our
dominant thoughts.
You are ripe when you have made this truth your own.

Also, be careful about what you dream.
Old age realizes the dreams of youth:
look at Dean Swift;
in his youth he built an asylum for the insane,
in his old age he was himself an inmate.

Jump! And pray your life to the fullest...
Pray like you have absolutely nothing to do.
Why are you so busy?
Who are you busy for?
You pursue pleasure with such breathless haste...
that you hurry pass it.
It seems essential, in all tasks, that you concentrate..
only on what is most significant and important.
Far from idleness being the root of all evil,
it is rather the only true good.

Pray like you are in love.
Just as in earthly life lovers long for the moment,
when they are able to breathe forth their love for each
other,
to let their souls blend in a soft whisper,
so long for the moment,

when in prayer you can, as it were,
breathe forth your love to God.

Prayer does not change God,
but it changes you who pray.
It is God who will fashion you..
God creates out of nothing.
Wonderful you say.
Yes, to be sure, but he does what is still more
wonderful:
He makes saints out of sinners.

If you do not jump, you will be bored!
Boredom is the root of all evil –
the despairing refusal to be oneself.
I begin with the principle that all men are bores.
Surely no one will prove himself so great a bore…
as to contradict me in this.
Since boredom advances and boredom is
the root of all evil,
no wonder, then, that the world goes backwards,
that evil spreads.

This can be traced back to the very
beginning of the world.
The gods were bored;
therefore they created human beings.
Gods created them to JUMP! -
The only way out from this boredom.

How do you become that Individual?

Do not let the world give you a name...
If that is not you.
Once they label you - they negate you.

Don't be afraid to becoming that Individual!
There is nothing with which every man is so afraid
as getting to know
how enormously much he is capable of
doing and becoming that Individual.

Don't expect world to understand you.
The world understand me so poorly that
they don't even understand
my complaint about them
not understanding me.

Don't fight with the world.
Quarrel with the world is completely fruitless,
whereas the quarrel with oneself is occasionally
fruitful...
and always, I have to admit, interesting.

To dare is to lose one's footing momentarily.
Not to dare is to lose oneself.
So, I dare you...
to become that Individual.

Jump!

MY PRAYER IN SØREN'S WORDS.

From your hand, O Wholly Other, I have received everything!

Even the knowledge and wisdom that my brother Søren has displayed.

You have stretched out your powerful hand and took me in at my foolishness.

I must confess, I have treated you like an 'object'!

But you have opened it, your gentle hand, and satisfied me with Søren's wisdom. And even if I feel that your arm is shortened by my misunderstanding of my brother's insights, then you increase my faith and my confidence, so that I may hold you, a 'subject', fast.

And if I feel that you have withdrew your hand from me, oh, then I know that it is only so because you have closed it, and you have closed it only in order to conceal the most abundant blessing within it, that you have closed it in order again to open it and satisfy everything with your eternal blessing.

In Jesus Name I pray,

Amen.

SUPPORT INFORMATION

I greet you in the Lord Jesus Christ.

Thank you so much for your love and support!

Robert Oh

◆Email: oikosbishop@mac.com

◆ Internet:
www.blesscambodia.com
* You can use PayPal from this site.

◆ USA :
Lifegiving Ministry
*Write the check to: 'Lifegiving Ministry' and Note: 'Cambodia Project'
PO Box 4885
Cerritos, CA 90703

◆ Korea :
KEB Hana Bank
Acct : 166-18-07737-7
Name : Oh Sukhwan